BRISKET DISHES COOKBOOK

100 Recipes, From Smoky BBQ Delights to Tender Oven Roasts

Richard Wood

TABLE OF CONTENTS

INTRODUCTION

This cookbook is designed to ignite your passion for cooking mouthwatering brisket dishes that will impress family and friends alike. Whether you're a seasoned pitmaster or a beginner in the kitchen, you'll find a collection of recipes that will guide you through the process of creating succulent, flavor-packed brisket dishes.

In this cookbook, we'll explore a variety of cooking techniques and flavor profiles to help you master the art of brisket preparation. From classic Texas-style BBQ to innovative fusion dishes, we'll showcase easy-to-follow recipes that will elevate your culinary skills and leave everyone asking for seconds.

So, fire up your grill or preheat your oven, and let's dive into the world of brisket, where smoky aromas, tender meat, and bold flavors await. Get ready to embark on a delicious journey that will have your taste buds dancing with joy.

BRISKET BREAKFAST

1.Brisket Hash

INGREDIENTS:

- 6 strips thick-cut bacon
- $\frac{1}{4}$ cup vegetable oil
- $2\frac{3}{4}$ cups frozen hash browns,thawed
- 1 medium red bell pepper,diced
- 1 large yellow onion,diced
- 2 cups chopped beef brisket
- 1 teaspoon garlic powder
- 1 teaspoon kosher salt
- $\frac{1}{2}$teaspoon ground black pepper
- $\frac{1}{4}$cup chopped green onions

INSTRUCTIONS

a) Place a large skillet over medium heat,then add in the bacon.Cook the bacon for about 5 minutes,or until it's nice and crisp.Remove the bacon from the skillet,but leave the rendered fat.Set the bacon to the side to cool.

b) Add the vegetable oil to the skillet,and let it heat up over medium heat.Once the oil is nice and hot,add in the hash browns.Cook the potatoes until they are golden and tender,usually about 7 minutes.

c) Add in the peppers and onions.Cook for 5 minutes.Then toss in the chopped beef brisket and sprinkle in the garlic powder,salt,and pepper.Stir the ingredients,and let cook for 7 more minutes.

d) Crumble the bacon that you cooked earlier,and toss it in the skillet along with the green onions.Mix the ingredients,and turn off the heat.Serve and enjoy with your favorite breakfast sides.

2.Brisket and Egg Breakfast Tacos

INGREDIENTS:

- 1 cup cooked brisket,shredded
- 4 large eggs
- 4 small flour tortillas
- 1/2 cup shredded cheddar cheese
- Salsa and sour cream for topping
- Salt and pepper to taste
- Chopped cilantro for garnish

INSTRUCTIONS:

a) Heat the brisket in a skillet over medium heat until heated through.
b) In a separate skillet,scramble the eggs until fully cooked.Season with salt and pepper.
c) Warm the flour tortillas in a dry skillet or microwave.
d) Place the brisket and scrambled eggs in the tortillas.
e) Top with shredded cheese,salsa,sour cream,and chopped cilantro.
f) Fold the tortillas and serve warm.

3. Brisket Breakfast Burrito

INGREDIENTS:

1 cup cooked brisket,sliced
4 large eggs
4 large flour tortillas
1/2 cup shredded Monterey Jack cheese
1/4 cup diced tomatoes
1/4 cup diced onions
1/4 cup chopped fresh cilantro
Salt and pepper to taste

INSTRUCTIONS:

In a skillet,heat the brisket over medium heat until heated through.
In a separate skillet,scramble the eggs until fully cooked.Season with salt and pepper.
Warm the flour tortillas in a dry skillet or microwave.
Place the brisket,scrambled eggs,shredded cheese,tomatoes,onions,and cilantro in the tortillas.
Fold the tortillas,tucking in the sides to form a burrito.
Serve warm.

4. Brisket and Potato Breakfast Casserole

INGREDIENTS:

2 cups cooked brisket,chopped

4 cups frozen shredded hash browns

1 cup shredded cheddar cheese

1/2 cup diced onions

1/2 cup diced bell peppers

6 large eggs

1 cup milk

1 teaspoon dried thyme

Salt and pepper to taste

INSTRUCTIONS:

Preheat the oven to 375°F(190°C)and grease a baking dish.

In a large bowl,combine the shredded hash browns,chopped brisket,shredded cheese,diced onions,and diced bell peppers.

In a separate bowl,whisk together the eggs,milk,dried thyme,salt,and pepper.

Pour the egg mixture over the brisket and potato mixture,stirring gently to combine.

Transfer the mixture to the greased baking dish and spread it evenly.

Bake for 35-40 minutes or until the top is golden brown and the casserole is set.

Allow the casserole to cool slightly before serving.

5.Brisket Breakfast Skillet

INGREDIENTS:

2 cups cooked brisket,shredded
4 large eggs
1 bell pepper,diced
1/2 onion,diced
2 cloves garlic,minced
1 tablespoon oil
Salt and pepper to taste
Fresh cilantro for garnish

INSTRUCTIONS:

Heat oil in a skillet over medium heat.Add onions,bell peppers,and garlic.Cook until softened.
Add the shredded brisket to the skillet and cook until heated through.
Create four wells in the skillet and crack an egg into each well.
Cover the skillet and cook until the eggs are cooked to your desired doneness.
Season with salt and pepper.
Garnish with fresh cilantro and serve hot.

6. Brisket Breakfast Quesadilla

INGREDIENTS:

- 1 cup cooked brisket,sliced
- 2 large flour tortillas
- 1/2 cup shredded Monterey Jack cheese
- 1/4 cup diced tomatoes
- 2 tablespoons chopped fresh cilantro
- Salt and pepper to taste
- Sour cream and salsa for dipping(optional)

INSTRUCTIONS:

a) Heat a large skillet over medium heat.
b) Place one tortilla in the skillet and sprinkle half of the shredded cheese evenly on top.
c) Layer the sliced brisket,diced tomatoes,and chopped cilantro on one half of the tortilla.
d) Season with salt and pepper.
e) Fold the tortilla in half,pressing down gently with a spatula.
f) Cook for 2-3 minutes on each side,until the cheese is melted and the tortilla is golden brown.
g) Remove from the skillet and repeat with the remaining tortilla and ingredients.
h) Cut each quesadilla into wedges and serve with sour cream and salsa if desired.

7.Brisket Breakfast Bowl

INGREDIENTS:

2 cups cooked brisket,chopped
4 cups cooked quinoa or rice
4 large eggs
1 avocado,sliced
1/4 cup diced red onion
1/4 cup chopped fresh cilantro
Hot sauce for topping(optional)
Salt and pepper to taste

INSTRUCTIONS:

Heat the chopped brisket in a skillet over medium heat until heated through.

In a separate skillet,fry the eggs to your desired doneness.Season with salt and pepper.

Divide the cooked quinoa or rice into four bowls.

Top each bowl with the heated brisket,fried eggs,avocado slices,diced red onion,and chopped cilantro.

Drizzle with hot sauce if desired.

Serve warm.

8. Brisket and Cheese Omelette

INGREDIENTS:

1 cup cooked brisket,chopped

4 large eggs

1/4 cup milk

1/2 cup shredded cheddar cheese

2 tablespoons chopped fresh chives

Salt and pepper to taste

Butter or oil for the pan

INSTRUCTIONS:

In a bowl,whisk together the eggs,milk,chopped brisket,shredded cheese,chopped chives,salt,and pepper.

Heat a non-stick skillet over medium heat and add butter or oil to the pan.

Pour the egg mixture into the skillet and cook until the edges start to set.

Using a spatula,gently lift the edges of the omelette to allow the uncooked eggs to flow to the bottom of the skillet.

Cook until the omelette is mostly set but still slightly runny on top.

Fold the omelette in half and continue cooking for another minute or until the cheese is melted and the eggs are fully cooked.

Slide the omelette onto a plate and serve hot.

9.Brisket Breakfast Wrap

INGREDIENTS:

1 cup cooked brisket,sliced

2 large flour tortillas

2 large eggs

1/2 cup shredded lettuce

1/4 cup diced tomatoes

2 tablespoons mayonnaise

Salt and pepper to taste

INSTRUCTIONS:

Heat the sliced brisket in a skillet over medium heat until heated through.

In a separate skillet,fry the eggs to your desired doneness.Season with salt and pepper.

Warm the flour tortillas in a dry skillet or microwave.

Spread the mayonnaise evenly over each tortilla.

Place the heated brisket,fried eggs,shredded lettuce,and diced tomatoes on one half of each tortilla.

Season with salt and pepper.

Fold the tortillas,tucking in the sides to form a wrap.

Serve warm.

BRISKET APPETIZERS

10.BBQ Beef Nachos

INGREDIENTS:

- 1 lb.shredded cooked beef brisket or roast
- 1/2 cup BBQ sauce
- 1 bag tortilla chips
- 1 cup shredded cheddar cheese
- 1 cup shredded Monterey Jack cheese
- 1/4 cup diced red onion
- 1/4 cup chopped fresh cilantro
- Sour cream for serving

INSTRUCTIONS

a) Preheat oven to 375°F.

b) In a bowl,mix the shredded beef with the BBQ sauce.

c) On a baking sheet,spread out the tortilla chips in a single layer.

d) Sprinkle the shredded cheeses over the chips,then top with the BBQ beef mixture.

e) Bake for 10-15 minutes,or until the cheese is melted and bubbly.

f) Top with diced red onion and chopped cilantro.Serve with sour cream.

11. Sweet Heat Burnt Ends

INGREDIENTS:

- 1(6-pound)brisket point
- 2 tablespoons yellow mustard
- 1 batch Sweet Brown Sugar Rub
- 2 tablespoons honey
- 1 cup barbecue sauce
- 2 tablespoons light brown sugar

INSTRUCTIONS:

Coat the point all over with mustard and season it with the rub.Using your hands,work the rub into the meat.

Place the point directly on the grill grate and smoke until its internal Smoke Temperature reaches 165°F.

Pull the brisket from the grill and wrap it entirely in aluminum foil or butcher paper.

Remove the point from the grill,unwrap it,and cut the meat into 1-inch cubes.Place the cubes in an aluminum pan and stir in the honey,barbecue sauce,and brown sugar.

Place the pan in the grill and smoke the beef cubes for 1 hour more,uncovered.Remove the burnt ends from the grill and serve immediately.

12. Brisket Stuffed Mushrooms

INGREDIENTS:

1 cup cooked brisket,finely chopped
20 large mushrooms
1/2 cup breadcrumbs
1/4 cup grated Parmesan cheese
2 tablespoons chopped fresh parsley
2 tablespoons olive oil
Salt and pepper to taste

INSTRUCTIONS:

Preheat the oven to 375°F(190°C).
Remove the stems from the mushrooms and set aside.
In a bowl,combine the chopped brisket,breadcrumbs,Parmesan cheese,chopped parsley,olive oil,salt,and pepper.
Stuff each mushroom cap with the brisket mixture.
Place the stuffed mushrooms on a baking sheet.
Bake in the preheated oven for about 15-20 minutes,or until the mushrooms are tender and the filling is heated through.
Remove from the oven and let cool slightly before serving.

13. Brisket Egg Rolls

INGREDIENTS:

1 cup cooked brisket,shredded
Egg roll wrappers
1/2 cup shredded cabbage
1/4 cup shredded carrots
2 green onions,thinly sliced
Soy sauce for dipping

INSTRUCTIONS:

In a bowl,combine the shredded brisket,shredded cabbage,shredded carrots,and sliced green onions.
Lay an egg roll wrapper flat on a clean surface.
Place a spoonful of the brisket mixture on one corner of the wrapper.
Roll the corner with the filling tightly,tucking in the sides as you go.
Moisten the edges of the wrapper with water to seal.
Repeat with the remaining wrappers and filling.
Heat oil in a deep skillet or fryer to 350°F(175°C).
Carefully place the egg rolls in the hot oil and fry until golden brown and crispy,about 2-3 minutes per side.
Remove from the oil and drain on a paper towel-lined plate.
Serve hot with soy sauce for dipping.

14.Brisket Quesadilla Bites

INGREDIENTS:

- 1 cup cooked brisket,chopped
- Mini flour tortillas
- Shredded cheese(cheddar,Monterey Jack,or a mix)
- Salsa and sour cream for dipping

INSTRUCTIONS:

a) Preheat a skillet over medium heat.
b) Place a mini tortilla in the skillet and sprinkle shredded cheese evenly on top.
c) Add a spoonful of chopped brisket to one half of the tortilla.
d) Fold the tortilla in half and press down gently with a spatula.
e) Cook for 2-3 minutes on each side,until the cheese is melted and the tortilla is golden brown.
f) Remove from the skillet and let cool slightly.
g) Repeat with the remaining tortillas and ingredients.
h) Cut each quesadilla into bite-sized triangles.
i) Serve with salsa and sour cream for dipping.

15.Brisket-Stuffed Jalapenos

INGREDIENTS:

- 12 jalapeno peppers
- 1 cup cooked brisket,finely chopped
- 1/2 cup cream cheese,softened
- 1/4 cup shredded cheddar cheese
- 1/4 teaspoon garlic powder
- 1/4 teaspoon onion powder
- Salt and pepper to taste
- Bacon slices(optional)

INSTRUCTIONS:

a) Preheat the oven to 400°F(200°C).
b) Cut the jalapenos in half lengthwise and remove the seeds and membranes.
c) In a bowl,combine the chopped brisket,cream cheese,shredded cheddar cheese,garlic powder,onion powder,salt,and pepper.
d) Spoon the brisket mixture into each jalapeno half,filling them evenly.
e) If desired,wrap each stuffed jalapeno half with a slice of bacon and secure with a toothpick.
f) Place the stuffed jalapenos on a baking sheet.
g) Bake in the preheated oven for about 15-20 minutes,or until the jalapenos are softened and the cheese is melted and bubbly.
h) Remove from the oven and let cool slightly before serving.

16. Brisket Crostini

INGREDIENTS:

Baguette,sliced into thin rounds
1 cup cooked brisket,thinly sliced
1/2 cup caramelized onions
1/4 cup crumbled blue cheese
Fresh thyme leaves for garnish

INSTRUCTIONS:

Preheat the oven to 375°F(190°C).
Arrange the baguette slices on a baking sheet.
Toast the baguette slices in the preheated oven for about 5-7 minutes,or until they are crispy and lightly browned.
Remove from the oven and let cool slightly.
Top each baguette slice with a few slices of brisket,a spoonful of caramelized onions,and a sprinkle of crumbled blue cheese.
Return the topped crostini to the oven for another 5 minutes,or until the cheese is melted.
Remove from the oven and let cool slightly before serving.
Garnish with fresh thyme leaves.

17. Brisket-Stuffed Potato Skins

INGREDIENTS:

4 large russet potatoes
1 cup cooked brisket,shredded
1/2 cup shredded cheddar cheese
1/4 cup sour cream
2 green onions,thinly sliced
Salt and pepper to taste

INSTRUCTIONS:

Preheat the oven to 400°F(200°C).
Scrub the potatoes clean and pierce them with a fork in several places.
Place the potatoes on a baking sheet and bake in the preheated oven for about 50-60 minutes,or until they are tender when pierced with a fork.
Remove the potatoes from the oven and let cool slightly.
Cut each potato in half lengthwise and scoop out the flesh,leaving a thin layer attached to the skin.
In a bowl,mix the shredded brisket,shredded cheddar cheese,sour cream,sliced green onions,salt,and pepper.
Spoon the brisket mixture evenly into the potato skins.
Return the filled potato skins to the oven and bake for another 15-20 minutes,or until the cheese is melted and bubbly.
Remove from the oven and let cool slightly before serving.

18. Brisket-Stuffed Mini Peppers

INGREDIENTS:

12 mini sweet peppers
1 cup cooked brisket,finely chopped
1/2 cup cream cheese,softened
1/4 cup shredded pepper jack cheese
1/4 teaspoon chili powder
1/4 teaspoon cumin
Salt and pepper to taste
Fresh cilantro for garnish

INSTRUCTIONS:

Preheat the oven to 375°F(190°C).
Cut the mini peppers in half lengthwise and remove the seeds and membranes.
In a bowl,combine the chopped brisket,cream cheese,shredded pepper jack cheese,chili powder,cumin,salt,and pepper.
Spoon the brisket mixture into each mini pepper half,filling them evenly.
Place the stuffed mini peppers on a baking sheet.
Bake in the preheated oven for about 12-15 minutes,or until the peppers are softened and the filling is heated through.
Remove from the oven and let cool slightly before serving.
Garnish with fresh cilantro.

SANDWICHES, BURGERS AND WRAPS

19.Green chile smoked brisket burritos

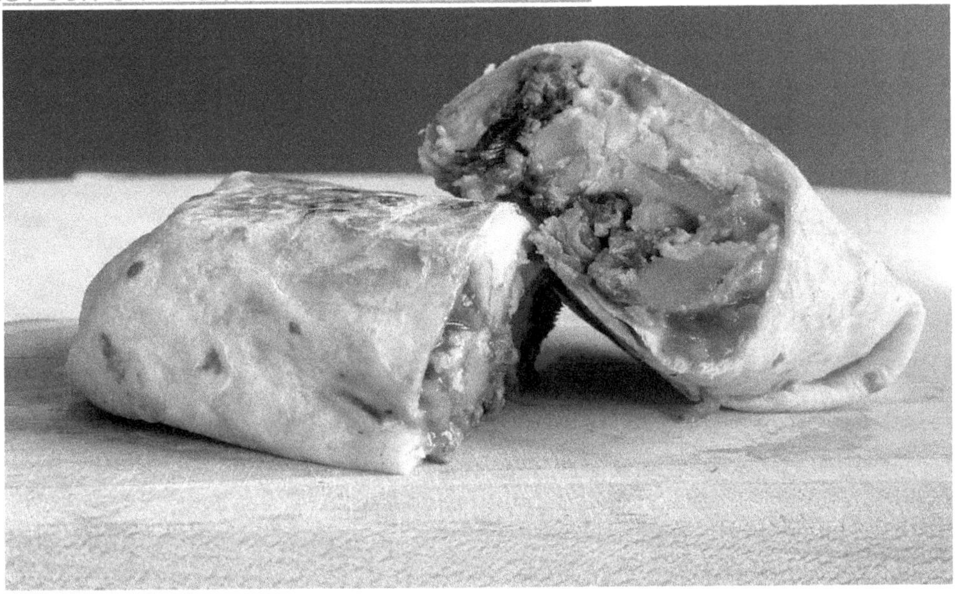

INGREDIENTS:

- 10 ounces Green chiles;diced
- 1 pint Kentucky Fried Chicken gravy
- 1 large Bell pepper;chopped
- 1 large Onion;chopped
- 1 cup Good salsa
- 1½pounds Smoked beef brisket;shredded
- 1 tablespoon Garlic;powder
- Salt to taste
- 16 Large flour tortillas
- 1 pounds Monterey Jack Cheese;shredded

INSTRUCTIONS:

a) In a large sauce pan or Dutch oven,sautébell pepper,onion,and green chiles with garlic powder in about 3 tablespoons of oil.

b) When onions and bell peppers are tender,add brisket,salsa,and gravy.

c) Cook over low heat for 30 minutes,stirring occasionally.Sample often.

d) Spoon meat mixture and cheese onto flour tortilla and wrap.

20.English Muffin Brisket Sandwich

INGREDIENTS:

1 cup cooked brisket,sliced

2 large eggs

2 English muffins,split and toasted

4 slices of cheddar cheese

Salt and pepper to taste

Ketchup or hot sauce(optional)

INSTRUCTIONS:

Heat the brisket in a skillet over medium heat until heated through.

In a separate skillet,fry the eggs to your desired doneness.Season with salt and pepper.

Place the slices of cheddar cheese on the toasted English muffins.

Layer the brisket and fried eggs on the cheese.

Top with ketchup or hot sauce if desired.

Place the remaining half of the English muffins on top to complete the sandwich.

Serve warm.

21. Slow-braised beef po'boy with gravy

INGREDIENTS:

- 1.4kg beef brisket
- 4 garlic cloves,sliced
- 2 tablespoons vegetable oil
- 1 large onion,finely diced
- 2 carrots,finely diced
- 500ml beef stock
- 250ml red wine
- 2-3 thyme sprigs
- 1 tablespoon corn flour
- Salt and freshly ground black pepper

TO SERVE

- 2 large baguettes,each cut into 3-4 pieces Little Gem lettuce,separated into leaves 3 large tomatoes,sliced
- 3-4 gherkins,sliced lengthways
- 2-3 tablespoons mayonnaise

INSTRUCTIONS:

a) Preheat the oven to 140°C/120°C Fan/Gas Mark 1.Take a small,sharp knife and pierce deep slits all over the beef.

b) Poke the garlic slices well into the slits,ensuring they are completely hidden within the meat so they won't fall out and burn when you are browning the beef.

c) Season generously all over with salt and pepper.

d) Add half the oil to a deep flameproof casserole dish-a heavy cast-iron dish is ideal-and set over a high heat.When the oil is smoking hot,add the beef and brown well all over-the deep caramelization adds much in terms of flavor,so do get a bit of color into it.

e) Remove to a plate,reduce the heat to low and add the remaining oil to the casserole dish,followed by the onion and carrot,stirring to soften a little for a couple of minutes.Return the beef to the pan along with any juices,then pour in the beef stock and red wine and tuck in the thyme.

f) Bring to a simmer then cover with a tight-fitting lid and slide into the oven.

g) Allow to cook very slowly for around 6-8 hours,turning the joint every couple of hours if you can to ensure even cooking,until it is really tender.You can test whether it's ready by trying to tease the meat apart with a fork-it should give easily;if not,cook for a little longer.

h) Turn off the oven.Lift the meat from the casserole dish and set aside on a plate in the oven to keep warm.Place 2 tablespoons of the cooking sauce into a heatproof glass and set aside to cool.Set the casserole dish on the hob over a high heat and boil for about 10 minutes until the sauce is reduced by half.

i) Stir the cornflour into the cooled reserved juices until you have a smooth paste.Pour into the dish and stir until the sauce thickens.Turn off the heat.

j) Remove the beef from the oven and cut into thick slices,dropping them into the gravy as you go and stirring to coat.

k) To serve,slice each piece of bread through the middle and open out,but leave top and bottom hinged together.Add a few slices of beef to each,plus a little sauce.

l) Top with lettuce,tomato and gherkin slices and finish with a little mayonnaise.Serve immediately.

22. Brisket Sliders

INGREDIENTS:

1 cup cooked brisket,shredded

Mini slider buns

BBQ sauce

Pickles or coleslaw for topping(optional)

INSTRUCTIONS:

Heat the shredded brisket in a skillet over medium heat until heated through.

Split the slider buns and lightly toast them.

Place a spoonful of heated brisket on the bottom half of each slider bun.

Drizzle BBQ sauce over the brisket.

Top with pickles or coleslaw if desired.

Place the top half of the slider bun on top.

Secure with a toothpick if needed.

Serve warm.

23. Brisket Sandwich with Caramelized Onions

INGREDIENTS:

1 cup cooked brisket,sliced
Ciabatta or your favorite bread
Caramelized onions(sliced onions cooked in butter until golden brown)
Dijon mustard
Arugula or your preferred greens

INSTRUCTIONS:

Spread Dijon mustard on one side of the bread slices.
Layer the sliced brisket,caramelized onions,and arugula on top.
Top with the other slice of bread.
Cut the sandwich in half if desired and serve.

24. BBQ Brisket Burger

INGREDIENTS:

1/2 pound ground beef
1/2 cup cooked brisket,chopped
2 tablespoons BBQ sauce
Hamburger buns
Cheese slices(optional)
Lettuce,tomatoes,onions,pickles(optional toppings)

INSTRUCTIONS:

In a bowl,mix together the ground beef,chopped brisket,and BBQ sauce until well combined.
Form the mixture into patties.
Grill the burgers over medium-high heat for about 4-5 minutes per side,or until cooked to your desired doneness.
If using cheese,place a slice on each burger during the last minute of grilling to melt.
Toast the hamburger buns on the grill if desired.
Assemble the burgers with your preferred toppings.
Serve the BBQ brisket burgers hot.

25. Brisket Reuben Sandwich

INGREDIENTS:

1 cup cooked brisket,thinly sliced
Rye bread
Swiss cheese
Sauerkraut,drained
Thousand Island dressing
Butter

INSTRUCTIONS:

Heat a skillet over medium heat.
Spread Thousand Island dressing on one side of each slice of rye bread.
Layer the sliced brisket,Swiss cheese,and sauerkraut on one slice of bread.
Top with the other slice of bread,dressing side down.
Spread butter on the outside of each slice of bread.
Place the sandwich in the skillet and cook until the bread is toasted and the cheese is melted,about 3-4 minutes per side.
Remove from the skillet,slice if desired,and serve hot.

26.Brisket and Blue Cheese Wrap

INGREDIENTS:

1 cup cooked brisket,sliced
Flour tortillas
Blue cheese crumbles
Sliced red onions
Baby spinach or mixed greens
Balsamic glaze or dressing

INSTRUCTIONS:

Lay a flour tortilla flat on a clean surface.
Place the sliced brisket,blue cheese crumbles,sliced red onions,and baby spinach or mixed greens in the center of the tortilla.
Drizzle with balsamic glaze or dressing.
Fold in the sides of the tortilla and roll it up tightly.
Slice the wrap in half if desired and serve.

27. Brisket Philly Cheesesteak Sandwich

INGREDIENTS:

1 cup cooked brisket,thinly sliced
Hoagie rolls or sub rolls
Sliced bell peppers
Sliced onions
Provolone cheese
Salt and pepper to taste
Mayonnaise or mustard(optional)

INSTRUCTIONS:

Heat a skillet over medium heat.
Add the sliced bell peppers and onions to the skillet and cook until softened.
Push the vegetables to one side of the skillet and add the sliced brisket to the other side.
Season with salt and pepper and cook until the brisket is heated through.
Place a few slices of provolone cheese on top of the brisket and vegetables.
Cover the skillet and let the cheese melt.
Split the hoagie rolls or sub rolls and spread mayonnaise or mustard on one side if desired.
Spoon the brisket,vegetables,and melted cheese onto the rolls.
Serve the brisket Philly cheesesteak sandwiches hot.

28.Grilled Brisket Quesadillas

INGREDIENTS:

4-5 pounds beef brisket,sliced into thin strips
Salt and pepper to taste
Flour tortillas
Shredded cheese(such as cheddar or Monterey Jack)
Sliced jalapenos(optional)
Guacamole,salsa,sour cream for serving

INSTRUCTIONS:

Preheat your grill to medium heat.
Season the brisket strips with salt and pepper.
Place the seasoned brisket strips on the grill and close the lid.
Grill for about 8-10 minutes,turning the brisket occasionally,or until the brisket is cooked to your desired level of doneness.
Remove the brisket from the grill and let it rest for a few minutes.
On one half of a flour tortilla,layer some shredded cheese,grilled brisket strips,sliced jalapenos(if using),and more shredded cheese.
Fold the tortilla in half to create a quesadilla.
Repeat the process with the remaining tortillas and filling.
Place the quesadillas on the grill and grill for about 2-3 minutes on each side,or until the tortillas are toasted and the cheese is melted.
Remove the quesadillas from the grill and let them cool slightly.
Slice the quesadillas into wedges and serve with guacamole,salsa,and sour cream.

29. Brisket Banh Mi Sandwich

INGREDIENTS:

1 cup cooked brisket,thinly sliced
Baguette or French bread
Pickled carrots and daikon radish
Fresh cilantro
Sliced cucumbers
Jalapeno slices(optional)
Sriracha or mayonnaise(optional)

INSTRUCTIONS:

Slice the baguette or French bread lengthwise.
If desired,spread Sriracha or mayonnaise on one or both sides of the bread.
Layer the sliced brisket,pickled carrots and daikon radish,fresh cilantro,sliced cucumbers,and jalapeno slices on one side of the bread.
Close the sandwich with the other side of the bread.
Cut the banh mi sandwich into individual servings if desired and serve.

30. Brisket Wrap with Avocado and Bacon

INGREDIENTS:

1 cup cooked brisket,sliced
Flour tortillas
Sliced avocado
Cooked bacon slices
Shredded lettuce
Tomato slices
Ranch dressing

INSTRUCTIONS:

Lay a flour tortilla flat on a clean surface.
Layer the sliced brisket,sliced avocado,cooked bacon slices,shredded lettuce,and tomato slices in the center of the tortilla.
Drizzle with ranch dressing.
Fold in the sides of the tortilla and roll it up tightly.
Slice the wrap in half if desired and serve.

31. Brisket and Pimento Cheese Sandwich

INGREDIENTS:

1 cup cooked brisket,sliced
Sourdough bread or your preferred bread
Pimento cheese spread
Arugula or your preferred greens

INSTRUCTIONS:

Spread a layer of pimento cheese spread on one side of each bread slice.
Layer the sliced brisket and arugula on top of the pimento cheese.
Top with the other slice of bread.
Cut the sandwich in half if desired and serve.

32. Brisket and Mushroom Melt

INGREDIENTS:

1 cup cooked brisket,sliced
Ciabatta or your preferred bread
Sliced mushrooms
Sliced onions
Swiss cheese
Butter

INSTRUCTIONS:

Heat a skillet over medium heat.
Add butter to the skillet and sautéthe sliced mushrooms and onions until they are tender and caramelized.
Remove the mushrooms and onions from the skillet and set aside.
In the same skillet,heat the sliced brisket until heated through.
Split the ciabatta bread or your preferred bread and lightly toast it.
Spread butter on one side of each bread slice.
Layer the heated brisket,sautéed mushrooms and onions,and Swiss cheese on one side of the bread.
Top with the other slice of bread,buttered side out.
Place the sandwich in the skillet and cook until the bread is toasted and the cheese is melted,about 3-4 minutes per side.
Remove from the skillet,slice if desired,and serve hot.

33. Brisket Wrap with Chipotle Mayo

INGREDIENTS:

1 cup cooked brisket,sliced
Flour tortillas
Chipotle mayo(mix mayonnaise with adobo sauce from canned chipotle peppers)
Sliced avocado
Thinly sliced red onion
Mixed greens

INSTRUCTIONS:

Lay a flour tortilla flat on a clean surface.
Spread chipotle mayo on one side of the tortilla.
Layer the sliced brisket,sliced avocado,thinly sliced red onion,and mixed greens in the center of the tortilla.
Fold in the sides of the tortilla and roll it up tightly.
Slice the wrap in half if desired and serve.

SOUPS, CURRY, AND CHILI

34. Venison Brisket Chili

INGREDIENTS:

- $\frac{1}{2}$lb.pinto or red beans
- 4 lbs.coarsely chopped venison
- 1$\frac{1}{2}$t.cumin seed
- $\frac{1}{2}$c.chopped suet or sowbelly cut in julienne strips
- 6 good-size onions,chopped
- 2-4 cloves garlic,minced
- 1 t.oregano
- 3 T.fresh chili powder
- 1 large can Italian peeled tomatoes
- 1 small can green chilies
- Salt and pepper
- Dash of Tabasco sauce(optional)
- 2 T.instant masa harina or Polenta

INSTRUCTIONS:

a) Wash the beans,cover with fresh cold water,bring to boil,and simmer 2 minutes;let stand,tightly covered,1 hour.Prepare meat(stewing cuts are best if fat-free)by cutting into 1-inch cubes.

b) Put cumin seeds in a skillet over medium heat and keep them moving until they smoke and turn toast-colored;then spread them on a flat surface and crush with a rolling pin.Now melt the suet or sowbelly in a large skillet;you may substitute enough vegetable oil or other shortening to coat the bottom of the pan,but you'll lose meaty flavor.

c) As soon as the fat is rendered or begins to sizzle add pieces of meat a few at a time and sear,turning cubes to seal all sides.

d) Lower heat and add onions and garlic,stirring occasionally until onions are translucent.Add parched cumin seed,oregano,and the freshest chili powder you can get;stir to coat meat with seasonings,add tomatoes and green chilies,and bring to boiling point,then reduce heat to simmer.

e) Bring the soaking beans to a boil again and allow to bubble almost imperceptibly until they are tender-30 minutes to an hour,depending upon beans.

f) Meanwhile watch the meat mixture to see that it is not getting too dry,adding water or stock as necessary to maintain a rather fluid consistency.Taste for seasoning,adding salt and pepper if necessary,and a dash of Tabasco as your taste buds decree.

g) After about 1½hours(time will depend upon quality and toughness of venison cuts)sample the meat;if tender skim off the excess grease-or refrigerate overnight to let the fat coagulate for easy removal.Add masa harina for thickening.

h) Then combine chili with cooked beans,bring back to simmering point,and allow flavors to meld for another 30 minutes.

35. Beef Brisket and Tripe Broth Soup

INGREDIENTS:

- 1 scallion,chopped
- 1 packet of oxtail bones including meat
- Seasoning to taste
- $1\frac{1}{2}$gallons water

INSTRUCTIONS:

a) Add the oxtail to a bowl containing water and leave it to soak,removing the excess blood,change the water 2-3 times.

b) When ready add the bones to a large pot and cover them with $1\frac{1}{2}$gallons of water.

c) Put on the stove and cook 6 hours'minimum,the longer you cook the better the taste and meat.

d) While it cooks,keep skimming off the oil that appears on top,keep the water level to around 1 gallon while cooking.

e) Once done the color should be creamy looking.

f) Correct the seasoning.

g) Serve in bowls with the oxtail and scatter the chopped scallions over the top.

36. Brisket and beet soup

INGREDIENTS:

- 4 mediums Tomatoes
- 4 tablespoons Butter
- 1 cup Onions;finely chopped
- 2 Garlic cloves,peeled;finely chopped
- 1 pounds Beets,trimmed of leaves,peeled,coarsely grated
- ½Celery root,peeled;coarsely grated
- 1 Parsley root,peeled;coarsely grated
- 1 Parsnip,peeled;coarsely grated
- ½teaspoon Sugar
- ¼cup Red wine vinegar
- 1 tablespoon Salt
- 2 quarts Beef stock,fresh or canned
- 1 pounds Boiling potatoes,peeled;cut in 1 1/2-inch chunks
- 1 pounds Cabbage,cored;coarsely shredded
- 1 pounds Boiled brisket,or 1 lb.boiled ham,cut in 1-inch chunks
- 3 tablespoons Parsley;finely chopped
- ½pint Sour cream

INSTRUCTIONS:

a) Drop the tomatoes into boiling water for 15 seconds.Run them under cold water and peel them.Cut out the stem,then slice them in half crosswise.

b) Squeeze the halves gently to remove the juices and seeds then chop them coarsely and set aside.

c) In a 10-to 12-inch skillet or casserole,melt the butter over moderate heat,Add the onions and garlic and,stirring frequently,cook 6 to 8 minutes,or until they are soft and lightly colored.Stir in the beets,celery root,parsley root,parsnip,half the tomatoes,the sugar,vinegar,salt and $1\frac{1}{2}$cups of the stock.Bring to a boil over high heat,then partially cover the pot and lower the heat.Simmer for 40 minutes.

d) Meanwhile,pour the remaining stock into a 6-8-qt casserole and add the potatoes and cabbage.Bring to a boil,then simmer partially covered for 20 minutes,or until the potatoes are tender but not falling apart.

e) When the vegetable mixture has cooked its allotted time,add it to the casserole with the remaining tomatoes and the meat.Simmer partially covered for 10 to 15 minutes,until the borscht is heated.

f) Taste for seasoning.Pour into a tureen,sprinkle with parsley and serve accompanied by sour cream.

37. Brisket Vegetable Soup

INGREDIENTS:

1 cup cooked brisket,chopped
4 cups beef broth
1 onion,diced
2 carrots,sliced
2 celery stalks,sliced
2 cloves garlic,minced
1 bay leaf
1 teaspoon dried thyme
Salt and pepper to taste
Chopped fresh parsley for garnish

INSTRUCTIONS:

In a large pot,heat some oil over medium heat.
Add the diced onion,sliced carrots,sliced celery,and minced garlic.Sautéuntil the vegetables are softened.
Add the chopped brisket,beef broth,bay leaf,dried thyme,salt,and pepper to the pot.
Bring the soup to a boil,then reduce the heat and simmer for about 20-30 minutes,allowing the flavors to meld together.
Remove the bay leaf before serving.
Garnish with chopped fresh parsley and serve hot.

38. Brisket and Barley Soup

INGREDIENTS:

1 cup cooked brisket,chopped
4 cups beef broth
1 onion,diced
2 carrots,diced
2 celery stalks,diced
1 cup pearl barley
2 cloves garlic,minced
1 bay leaf
1 teaspoon dried thyme
Salt and pepper to taste
Chopped fresh parsley for garnish

INSTRUCTIONS:

In a large pot,heat some oil over medium heat.
Add the diced onion,diced carrots,diced celery,and minced garlic.Sautéuntil the vegetables are softened.
Add the chopped brisket,beef broth,pearl barley,bay leaf,dried thyme,salt,and pepper to the pot.
Bring the soup to a boil,then reduce the heat to low and cover.
Simmer for about 45 minutes to 1 hour,or until the barley is tender and the flavors have melded together.
Remove the bay leaf before serving.
Garnish with chopped fresh parsley and serve hot.

39.Brisket Curry

INGREDIENTS:

1 cup cooked brisket,thinly sliced
1 onion,diced
3 cloves garlic,minced
1 tablespoon grated ginger
2 tablespoons curry powder
1 can(14 ounces)coconut milk
1 cup beef broth
2 potatoes,peeled and diced
1 carrot,sliced
Salt and pepper to taste
Fresh cilantro for garnish
Cooked rice or naan bread for serving

INSTRUCTIONS:

In a large pot or deep skillet,heat some oil over medium heat.

Add the diced onion,minced garlic,and grated ginger.Sautéuntil the onions are translucent.

Add the curry powder and cook for a minute until fragrant.

Add the sliced brisket,coconut milk,beef broth,diced potatoes,and sliced carrot.

Season with salt and pepper to taste.

Bring the mixture to a simmer,then cover and cook for about 20-30 minutes,or until the vegetables are tender and the flavors have melded together.

Garnish with fresh cilantro and serve with cooked rice or naan bread.

40. Brisket and Black Bean Chili

INGREDIENTS:

1 cup cooked brisket,chopped

1 onion,diced

2 cloves garlic,minced

1 jalapeno pepper,seeded and diced

1 can(14 ounces)diced tomatoes

1 can(14 ounces)black beans,drained and rinsed

1 cup beef broth

1 tablespoon chili powder

1 teaspoon cumin

1 teaspoon paprika

Salt and pepper to taste

Optional toppings:shredded cheese,sour cream,chopped green onions,etc.

INSTRUCTIONS:

In a large pot,heat some oil over medium heat.

Add the diced onion,minced garlic,and diced jalapeno pepper.Sautéuntil the onions are translucent.

Add the chopped brisket,diced tomatoes,black beans,beef broth,chili powder,cumin,paprika,salt,and pepper to the pot.

Bring the chili to a boil,then reduce the heat and simmer for about 30 minutes,allowing the flavors to meld together.

Adjust the seasoning if needed.

Serve the brisket and black bean chili hot with your desired toppings.

41.Brisket and Sweet Potato Stew

INGREDIENTS:

1 cup cooked brisket,chopped
1 onion,diced
2 cloves garlic,minced
2 sweet potatoes,peeled and diced
2 carrots,sliced
4 cups beef broth
1 bay leaf
1 teaspoon dried thyme
Salt and pepper to taste
Chopped fresh parsley for garnish

INSTRUCTIONS:

In a large pot,heat some oil over medium heat.
Add the diced onion and minced garlic.Sautéuntil the onions are translucent.
Add the chopped brisket,diced sweet potatoes,sliced carrots,beef broth,bay leaf,dried thyme,salt,and pepper to the pot.
Bring the stew to a boil,then reduce the heat and simmer for about 30-40 minutes,or until the sweet potatoes and carrots are tender.
Remove the bay leaf before serving.
Garnish with chopped fresh parsley and serve hot.

42. Brisket Tortilla Soup

INGREDIENTS:

1 cup cooked brisket,shredded

1 onion,diced

2 cloves garlic,minced

1 jalapeno pepper,seeded and diced

1 can(14 ounces)diced tomatoes

4 cups chicken broth

1 teaspoon chili powder

1 teaspoon cumin

1/2 teaspoon paprika

Salt and pepper to taste

Tortilla strips,avocado slices,lime wedges,and chopped cilantro for garnish

INSTRUCTIONS:

In a large pot,heat some oil over medium heat.

Add the diced onion,minced garlic,and diced jalapeno pepper.Sautéuntil the onions are translucent.

Add the shredded brisket,diced tomatoes,chicken broth,chili powder,cumin,paprika,salt,and pepper to the pot.

Bring the soup to a boil,then reduce the heat and simmer for about 15-20 minutes,allowing the flavors to meld together.

Adjust the seasoning if needed.

Serve the brisket tortilla soup hot,garnished with tortilla strips,avocado slices,lime wedges,and chopped cilantro.

43. Brisket and Lentil Soup

INGREDIENTS:

1 cup cooked brisket,chopped

1 onion,diced

2 cloves garlic,minced

1 carrot,diced

1 celery stalk,diced

1 cup dried lentils,rinsed and drained

4 cups beef broth

1 bay leaf

1 teaspoon dried thyme

Salt and pepper to taste

Chopped fresh parsley for garnish

INSTRUCTIONS:

In a large pot,heat some oil over medium heat.

Add the diced onion,minced garlic,diced carrot,and diced celery.Sautéuntil the vegetables are softened.

Add the chopped brisket,dried lentils,beef broth,bay leaf,dried thyme,salt,and pepper to the pot.

Bring the soup to a boil,then reduce the heat and simmer for about 30-40 minutes,or until the lentils are tender and the flavors have melded together.

Remove the bay leaf before serving.

Garnish with chopped fresh parsley and serve hot.

44. Brisket and Corn Chowder

INGREDIENTS:

1 cup cooked brisket,chopped
1 onion,diced
2 cloves garlic,minced
2 potatoes,peeled and diced
2 cups corn kernels(fresh or frozen)
4 cups chicken broth
1 cup milk or cream
2 tablespoons flour
2 tablespoons butter
Salt and pepper to taste
Chopped fresh parsley or chives for garnish

INSTRUCTIONS:

In a large pot,melt the butter over medium heat.
Add the diced onion and minced garlic.Sautéuntil the onions are translucent.
Add the diced potatoes,corn kernels,and chicken broth to the pot.
Bring the chowder to a boil,then reduce the heat and simmer for about 15-20 minutes,or until the potatoes are tender.
In a small bowl,whisk together the flour and milk or cream until smooth.
Slowly pour the milk mixture into the chowder while stirring continuously.
Add the chopped brisket to the pot and stir to combine.
Simmer for an additional 5 minutes,or until the chowder has thickened slightly.
Season with salt and pepper to taste.

Garnish with chopped fresh parsley or chives and serve hot.

45. Brisket and Bean Stew

INGREDIENTS:

1 cup cooked brisket,chopped
1 onion,diced
2 cloves garlic,minced
1 bell pepper,diced
1 can(14 ounces)diced tomatoes
2 cans(14 ounces each)beans of your choice(such as black beans,kidney beans,or pinto beans),drained and rinsed
4 cups beef broth
1 teaspoon chili powder
1 teaspoon cumin
Salt and pepper to taste
Chopped fresh cilantro for garnish

INSTRUCTIONS:

In a large pot,heat some oil over medium heat.
Add the diced onion,minced garlic,and diced bell pepper.Sautéuntil the onions are translucent.
Add the chopped brisket,diced tomatoes,beans,beef broth,chili powder,cumin,salt,and pepper to the pot.
Bring the stew to a boil,then reduce the heat and simmer for about 20-30 minutes,allowing the flavors to meld together.
Adjust the seasoning if needed.
Serve the brisket and bean stew hot,garnished with chopped fresh cilantro.

46. Brisket and Mushroom Chili

INGREDIENTS:

1 cup cooked brisket,chopped
1 onion,diced
2 cloves garlic,minced
8 ounces mushrooms,sliced
1 can(14 ounces)diced tomatoes
1 can(14 ounces)kidney beans,drained and rinsed
1 cup beef broth
1 tablespoon chili powder
1 teaspoon cumin
1/2 teaspoon paprika
Salt and pepper to taste
Optional toppings:shredded cheese,sour cream,chopped green onions,etc.

INSTRUCTIONS:

In a large pot,heat some oil over medium heat.
Add the diced onion,minced garlic,and sliced mushrooms.Sautéuntil the onions are translucent and the mushrooms are browned.
Add the chopped brisket,diced tomatoes,kidney beans,beef broth,chili powder,cumin,paprika,salt,and pepper to the pot.
Bring the chili to a boil,then reduce the heat and simmer for about 30 minutes,allowing the flavors to meld together.
Adjust the seasoning if needed.
Serve the brisket and mushroom chili hot with your desired toppings.

MAIN COURSE

7.Country Beef Brisket

INGREDIENTS:

- 1 fresh beef brisket(2-1/2 to 3 pounds),trimmed

MARINADE:

- 1/2 cup soy sauce
- 1 can(10-1/2 ounces)condensed beef broth,undiluted
- 2 tablespoons plus 1-1/2 teaspoons lemon juice
- 1/2 teaspoon garlic powder
- Paprika

SEASONED BROTH:

- 1/4 cup cider vinegar
- 1/4 cup Worcestershire sauce
- 1/4 cup packed brown sugar
- 1/2 to 1 teaspoon Liquid Smoke,optional

INSTRUCTIONS:

a) Put the brisket in a shallow dish with a lid.Mix the lemon juice,garlic powder,soy sauce,and broth.

b) Pour it over the brisket.Put a cover on and place in refrigerator overnight.Drain;remove 1 cup of marinade and discard the rest.Put the marinade reserved back in the refrigerator.

c) Put the meat in a shallow baking dish and shake paprika on.Put foil tightly on top.Bake in a 325-degree oven until brisket is tender,3 hours.Let stand until cool and place in refrigerator.

d) Throw out the cooking juices.When good and cold,cut meat into slices and put back in the baking dish.In a pot,mix reserved marinade and ingredients for seasoned broth.Gently boil for 10 minutes and dump over brisket.

e) Bake covered in a 325-degree oven until heated,1 hour.

48. Jamaican Jerk Brisket

INGREDIENTS:

- 12 pound brisket
- 3 cups jerk seasoning
- 5 pimento leaves or bay leaves
- 2 tablespoons allspice berries

INSTRUCTIONS:

a) Using a sharp knife,trim the brisket,leaving a layer of fat at least 1/4 inch thick.Be careful not to over-trim.It's better to err on the side of too much fat than too little.Make a series of 1/2-inch-deep cuts on all sides of the meat using the tip of a paring knife,twisting the blade to widen the holes.

b) Using a rubber spatula,slather the brisket with jerk seasoning on all sides.Force it into the holes you made with the paring knife.Marinate,covered,in the refrigerator for at least 6 hours or overnight—the longer it marinates,the richer the flavor.

c) Fire up your smoker,cooker,or grill following the manufacturer's instructions and heat to 250°F.Add the wood as specified by the manufacturer.If using a water smoker,add the pimento leaves and allspice berries to the water pan.Otherwise,place these flavorings in a metal bowl or aluminum foil pan with 1 quart warm water and place the bowl in the smoker.

d) Scrape the excess jerk marinade off the brisket with a spatula.Place the brisket fat side up in the smoker.If using an offset smoker,position the thicker end toward the firebox.Cook the brisket until the outside is darkly browned and the internal temperature registers about 165°F on an instant-read thermometer,about 8

hours.Refuel your cooker as needed,following the manufacturer's instructions.
e) Remove the brisket from the smoker and tightly wrap it in butcher paper.Return it to the cooker.
f) Continue cooking until the internal temperature is around 205°F and the meat is very tender when tested,another 2 to 4 hours,or as needed.
g) Place the wrapped jerk brisket in an insulated cooler and let it rest for 1 to 2 hours.
h) Unwrap the brisket and transfer it to a welled cutting board.Pour any juices that accumulated in the butcher paper into a bowl.
i) Slice the brisket across the grain into 1/4-inch-thick slices.Layer the slices onto the toasted rolls,
j) if desired.Add any juices from the cutting board to the juices in the bowl,spoon them over the meat,and serve.

49. Beef and Potato

INGREDIENTS:

- 6 pounds(2.7 kg)corned beef brisket
- 10 cups water
- 2 tablespoons pickling spice(optional)
- 5 cups diced potato
- 2 cups carrots,cut into chunks
- 2 onions,diced

INSTRUCTIONS:

a) Trim your brisket to remove as much fat as possible,then cut it into bite-sized pieces.

b) Put water and pickling spice,if using,into a stockpot and bring it to a boil.

c) Layer potatoes,carrots,and onion in the bottom third of your wide-mouth quart jars.

d) Layer brisket on top of the potatoes and allow 1 inch of headspace.

e) Ladle spiced water into the jars,maintaining the inch of headspace.I strain the spices out,because they greatly intensify while this sits on the shelf.

f) Using a rubber spatula,remove any air pockets.

g) Wipe the rims of the jars with a paper towel dipped in vinegar,then put the lids on.

h) Process in a pressure canner at 11 PSI for 90 minutes,adjusting for altitude.

50.Mesquite-Smoked Brisket(Wrapped)

INGREDIENTS:

1(12-pound)full packer brisket

2 tablespoons yellow mustard

Salt

Freshly ground black pepper

INSTRUCTIONS:

Coat the brisket all over with mustard and season with salt and pepper.

Place the brisket directly on the grill grate and smoke until its internal Smoke Temperature reaches 160°F and the brisket has formed a dark bark.

Pull the brisket from the grill and wrap it entirely in aluminum foil or butcher paper.

Transfer the wrapped brisket to a calmer,cover the cooler,and let the brisket rest for 1 or 2 hours.

Remove the brisket from the more relaxed and unwrap it.

51.Braised brisket with five spices

INGREDIENTS:

- 8 ounces ginger,with skin
- 2 onions,halved
- 3 tablespoons vegetable oil
- 3 tablespoons of five-spice powder
- Kosher salt and ground pepper,
- 8 cups of beef broth
- Soy sauce,1 cup
- 4-pound brisket
- 1 cup light brown sugar
- Hoisin sauce,1 cup
- 10 cloves of garlic
- anise 3 stars
- 3 whole cloves
- 2 cinnamon sticks
- 1 bunch of scallions,chopped

INSTRUCTIONS:

a) Cook ginger and onions in a skillet for 8 minutes,stirring as necessary.
b) Heat oil using a Crockpot.
c) Season brisket with salt,pepper,and five-spice powder and brown for 6 minutes,flipping as necessary,until golden brown.
d) Deglaze the pan with 1 cup of liquid.
e) Transfer the ginger,onions,and brisket along with the remaining ingredients to the crockpot and cook on low for 3 hours.
f) Slice the brisket and serve with the braising liquid.

52.Corned beef brisket barbecue

INGREDIENTS:

- 3 pounds Corned beef brisket
- 6 moderates Baking potatoes
- 1 each Dry onion soup mix envelope
- $\frac{1}{2}$cup Butter,softened
- $\frac{1}{2}$cup Sugar
- $\frac{1}{4}$cup Vinegar
- 5 tablespoons Ready mustard
- 1 cup Sour cream
- $\frac{1}{4}$cup Milk

INSTRUCTIONS:

a) Pre-heat both sides of gas grill on HIGH for 10 minutes.Turn burners to moderate.Rinse corned beef;place in foil baking pan on cooking grids.Close hood and cook for 1$\frac{1}{2}$hours.

b) Scrub potatoes but do not peel;cut each potato into 3 or 4 length-wise segments.Set aside 3 Tablespoons of soup mix.;Mix together remaining mix and butter.Spread mixture on potato segments and re-assemble;wrap each potato in heavy foil;place on grill with corned beef.Cover hood and grill 45 to 60 minutes longer,rotating potatoes once.

c) In saucepan mix sugar,vinegar,3 Tablespoons mustard and dash of salt.Bring to boiling;stir up until sugar dissolves.Brush over corned beef last few minutes of grilling.Mix sour cream,milk,reserved soup mix and remaining mustard.Heat,stirring occasionally,but do not boil.

d) Segment meat across grain;serve with potatoes and sour cream sauce.

53.Pork Bo Kho

INGREDIENTS:

1¼lbs pork briskets
1 tablespoon ghee
½small onion,diced
1 tablespoon fresh ginger,grated
1 tablespoon red boat fish sauce
½large stalk lemongrass,cut into 3-inch lengths
½bay leaf
½cup diced tomatoes
½lb carrots,peeled and chopped
1 teaspoon Madras curry powder
1 tablespoon apple sauce
1 whole star anise
½cup bone broth
½teaspoon salt

INSTRUCTIONS:

Select'sauté'function on the instant pot and add the ghee to it.
Stir-fry the briskets in the pot in batches.
Transfer the briskets to a plate and put the onions into the pot.
Sautéthe onions for 3 minutes then add the ginger,carrots,dicedtomatoes,curry powder,red boat fish sauce,and the seared pork.
Stir in the lemongrass,bay leaf,broth,apple sauce and star anise.
Cook on"the'manual'function for 35 minutes at high pressure.
Release the pressure naturally for 30 minutes then remove the lid.

Serve immediately.

54. Brisket of beef over wild rice

INGREDIENTS:

- 2½pounds Fresh Beef Brisket
- 1 teaspoon Salt
- ¼teaspoon Garlic Powder
- 1 Bottle(12 oz)Beer
- 2 Med.Ripe Tomatoes,Sliced
- ½cup Diced Onion
- 1 teaspoon Pepper
- 1 Bottle(12 Oz)Chili Sauce
- Wild Rice Amandine
- Parsley Sprigs

INSTRUCTIONS:

a) Place beef brisket,fat side down,in deep roasting pan.Sprinkle brisket with onion,salt,pepper and garlic powder.Pour chili sauce over brisket.Cover tightly and cook in slow oven(325 degrees F.)for 3 hours.Pour beer over brisket.

b) Place brisket on large serving platter and surround with Wild Rice Amandine.

c) Garnish with sliced tomatoes and parsley.Slice brisket very thin and serve with hot cooking liquid.

5.Saucy Pork Brisket

INGREDIENTS:

- 4 lbs pork brisket,flat cut
- $\frac{1}{2}$teaspoon celery salt
- $\frac{1}{2}$teaspoon garlic salt
- $\frac{1}{2}$teaspoon Lowry's seasoned salt
- 2 tablespoons Worcestershire sauce
- 2 cups barbecue sauce
- 4 tablespoons liquid smoke
- 1 cup water

INSTRUCTIONS:

a) Season the pork brisket with salt,garlic salt,celery salt,liquid smoker and Worcestershire sauce.2.Marinate the seasoned pork overnight.
b) Add the barbecue sauce,water and marinated pork into the instant pot.
c) Select'manual'and cook for 60 minutes at high pressure.
d) After the beep,'natural release'the steam for 15 minutes.
e) Remove the lid and serve hot.

56. Beer and chile braised brisket

INGREDIENTS:

- 2 Cloves garlic;minced
- 2 teaspoons Ground cumin
- $\frac{1}{4}$teaspoon Cinnamon
- $\frac{1}{4}$cup Plus 1 Tbs.brown sugar
- 5 pounds Brisket
- 2 large Onions;cut into wedges
- 1 cup Dark beer;or stout
- 3 tablespoons Tomato paste
- 1 tablespoon Canned chipotle chiles
- 10 smalls Red potatoes;cut in half
- $\frac{1}{2}$pounds Baby carrots

INSTRUCTIONS:

a) Mix first 3 ingredients thoroughly.Rub brisket with spice mixture to cover and place on foil.

b) Place onion wedges over meat.Combine next 3 ingredients and remaining brown sugar in a bowl.Pour over meat.

c) Baste meat with pan juices and bake another hour.

d) Add potatoes and carrots to the pan.Bake about 1-$\frac{1}{2}$hours,uncovered.

CURED BRISKET

57. Beer salami

INGREDIENTS:

- 3 pounds Corned beef brisket,cubed
- 7 pounds Ham,cubed,fat included
- $1\frac{1}{2}$tablespoon black pepper
- 1 tablespoon Ground mace
- $1\frac{1}{2}$tablespoon Crushed mustard seed
- 2 teaspoons Garlic,finely minced
- 4 Feet large beef casings

INSTRUCTIONS:

a) Begin smoking at about 80 degrees and gradually raise the temperature to 160.This should take about 4 hours.Smoke an additional 2 hours.

b) Cool by dunking in a pot of cool(not cold)water for about 5 minutes until it is cool to the touch.Dry the salami thoroughly and store it in the refrigerator.

58. Classic Pastrami

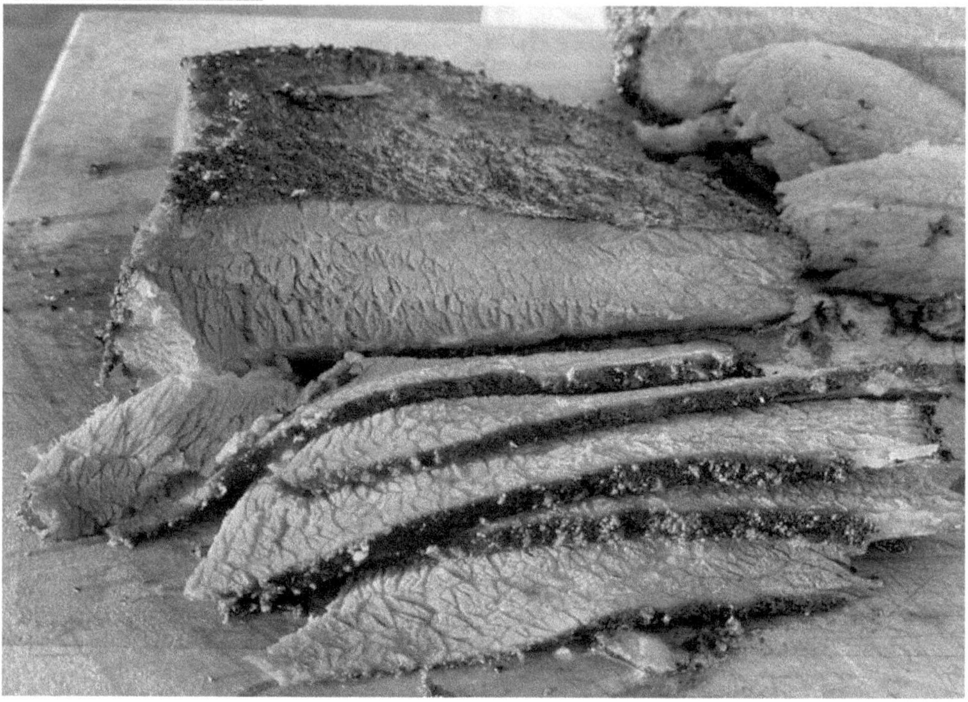

INGREDIENTS:

- Beef brisket,cut from the point
- Kosher salt-6$\frac{1}{2}$tablespoons
- Brown sugar-6 tablespoons
- Coriander seeds-$\frac{1}{4}$teaspoon
- Honey-1 tablespoon
- 3 bay leaves,chopped
- Garlic,peeled and chopped-1 teaspoon
- Cayenne pepper-$\frac{1}{4}$teaspoon
- Whole black peppercorns-$\frac{1}{4}$cup
- Brown sugar-1 tablespoon
- Coriander seeds-$\frac{1}{4}$cup
- Garlic powder-2 teaspoons
- Paprika-1 tablespoon
- Onion powder-2 teaspoons

INSTRUCTIONS:

a) Combine the kosher salt,brown sugar,coriander seeds,curing salt,honey,bay leaves,garlic,and cayenne pepper and transfer to a large container.
b) Add the meat to the cooled brine and weigh down with a plate.Set the meat aside for one week to brine.
c) In a bowl,combine the black peppercorns,brown sugar,coriander seeds,garlic powder,paprika,and onion powder.
d) Rub the mixture evenly over the outside of the meat.
e) Place the meat on the grill grate and cook for 4 hours.

59.Classic Corned Beef Brisket

INGREDIENTS:

- 4-5 pounds beef brisket
- 1 cup kosher salt
- 1/2 cup brown sugar
- 2 tablespoons pickling spices
- 6 cloves garlic,minced
- 2 tablespoons pink curing salt(optional)
- Water,enough to cover the brisket

INSTRUCTIONS:

a) In a large pot,combine kosher salt,brown sugar,pickling spices,minced garlic,and pink curing salt(if using).
b) Add enough water to cover the brisket and stir until the salt and sugar have dissolved.
c) Place the brisket in the brine mixture,ensuring it is completely submerged.
d) Cover the pot and refrigerate for 5-7 days,flipping the brisket once a day.
e) After the curing period,remove the brisket from the brine and rinse it under cold water to remove excess salt.
f) Place the brisket in a large pot and cover it with fresh water.
g) Bring the water to a boil,then reduce the heat and simmer for 3-4 hours,or until the brisket is tender.
h) Once cooked,slice the corned beef against the grain and serve.

60. Salt-Cured Brisket(Bresaola)

INGREDIENTS:

4-5 pounds beef brisket
1 cup kosher salt
1/2 cup granulated sugar
1 tablespoon black peppercorns,crushed
4 cloves garlic,minced
4 sprigs fresh rosemary,chopped
4 sprigs fresh thyme,chopped

INSTRUCTIONS:

In a bowl,combine kosher salt,granulated sugar,crushed black peppercorns,minced garlic,chopped rosemary,and chopped thyme.

Rub the salt mixture all over the brisket,ensuring it is evenly coated.

Place the brisket in a large resealable plastic bag or airtight container and refrigerate for 7-10 days,flipping the brisket once a day.

After the curing period,remove the brisket from the bag or container and rinse it under cold water to remove excess salt and herbs.

Pat the brisket dry with paper towels and hang it in a cool,well-ventilated place for 3-4 weeks,or until it has dried and developed a firm texture.

Once cured,slice the bresaola thinly and serve.

61. Dry-Cured Brisket

INGREDIENTS:

- 4-5 pounds beef brisket
- 1/4 cup kosher salt
- 1/4 cup brown sugar
- 1 tablespoon black peppercorns,crushed
- 1 tablespoon coriander seeds,crushed
- 1 tablespoon garlic powder
- 1 tablespoon onion powder
- 1 tablespoon paprika
- 1 tablespoon dried thyme
- 1 tablespoon dried rosemary

INSTRUCTIONS:

a) In a bowl,combine kosher salt,brown sugar,crushed black peppercorns,crushed coriander seeds,garlic powder,onion powder,paprika,dried thyme,and dried rosemary.
b) Rub the spice mixture all over the brisket,ensuring it is evenly coated.
c) Place the brisket in a resealable plastic bag or wrap it tightly in plastic wrap.Refrigerate for 7-10 days,flipping the brisket once a day.
d) After the curing period,remove the brisket from the bag or plastic wrap and rinse it under cold water to remove excess salt and spices.
e) Preheat your oven to 225°F(110°C).
f) Place the brisket on a rack set inside a roasting pan and roast for 6-8 hours,or until the internal temperature reaches 195°F(90°C)and the brisket is tender.
g) Once cooked,let the dry-cured brisket rest for a few minutes before slicing it against the grain.

SMOKED BRISKET

62. Unwrapped Texas Smoked Brisket

INGREDIENTS:

1(12-pound)full packer brisket
2 tablespoons yellow mustard
1 batch Espresso Brisket Rub
Worcestershire Mop and Spritz,for spritzing

INSTRUCTIONS:

a) Coat the brisket all over with mustard and season it with the rub.Using your hands,work the rub into the meat.Pour the mop into a spray bottle.
b) Place the brisket directly on the grill grate and smoke until its internal Smoke Temperature reaches 195°F,spritzing it every hour with the mop.
c) Pull the brisket from the grill and wrap it entirely in aluminum foil or butcher paper.Place the wrapped brisket in a more relaxed,cover the more relaxed,and let it rest for 1 or 2 hours.
d) Remove the brisket from the more relaxed and unwrap it.

3. Texan-Style Smoke Beef Brisket

INGREDIENTS:

- 1 whole packet brisket
- Sea salt-2 tablespoons
- Garlic powder-2 tablespoons
- black pepper-2 tablespoons

INSTRUCTIONS:

a) In a bowl,combine the rub ingredients,sea salt,garlic powder and black pepper.Rub the seasoning all over the brisket.

b) Arrange the meat on the smoker with the pointed end facing towards the primary heat source.Close the smoker lid and smoke for approximately 8 hours.

c) Wrap the meat,by folding the foil edge over edge to create a leaf-proof seal all the way around.Return the foil-wrapped brisket to the smoker,seam side facing downwards.

d) Close the smoker's lid and continue to cook at 225°F(110°C).This will take between 5-8 hours.

64. Smoked Brisket with Coffee Rub

INGREDIENTS:

8-10 pounds beef brisket
Salt and pepper to taste
1/4 cup finely ground coffee
2 tablespoons brown sugar
1 tablespoon paprika
1 tablespoon chili powder
1 tablespoon garlic powder
1 tablespoon onion powder
1 teaspoon cayenne pepper(optional)

INSTRUCTIONS:

Preheat your smoker to 225°F(110°C)and prepare it for indirect heat.
Trim any excess fat from the brisket,leaving about 1/4 inch of fat.
Season the brisket with salt and pepper.
In a bowl,combine the finely ground coffee,brown sugar,paprika,chili powder,garlic powder,onion powder,and cayenne pepper(if using).Mix well.
Rub the coffee spice mixture all over the brisket,making sure to coat all sides.
Place the brisket in the smoker,fat side up.
Close the smoker and let the brisket smoke for about 1.5 to 2 hours per pound,or until the internal temperature reaches around 195°F(90°C)to 203°F(95°C)and the brisket is tender.
Remove the brisket from the smoker and let it rest for at least 30 minutes.
Slice the brisket against the grain and serve.

65. Smoked Brisket with Mustard Rub

INGREDIENTS:

8-10 pounds beef brisket

Salt and pepper to taste

1/4 cup Dijon mustard

2 tablespoons brown sugar

1 tablespoon paprika

1 tablespoon chili powder

1 tablespoon garlic powder

1 tablespoon onion powder

INSTRUCTIONS:

Preheat your smoker to 225°F(110°C)and prepare it for indirect heat.

Trim any excess fat from the brisket,leaving about 1/4 inch of fat.

Season the brisket with salt and pepper.

In a bowl,combine the Dijon mustard,brown sugar,paprika,chili powder,garlic powder,and onion powder.Mix well.

Rub the mustard mixture all over the brisket,making sure to coat all sides.

Place the brisket in the smoker,fat side up.

Close the smoker and let the brisket smoke for about 1.5 to 2 hours per pound,or until the internal temperature reaches around 195°F(90°C)to 203°F(95°C)and the brisket is tender.

Remove the brisket from the smoker and let it rest for at least 30 minutes.

Slice the brisket against the grain and serve.

6. Smoked Brisket with Maple Glaze

INGREDIENTS:

8-10 pounds beef brisket
Salt and pepper to taste
1/4 cup maple syrup
2 tablespoons Dijon mustard
2 tablespoons apple cider vinegar
2 tablespoons brown sugar
1 tablespoon paprika
1 tablespoon garlic powder
1 tablespoon onion powder
1 teaspoon cayenne pepper(optional)

INSTRUCTIONS:

Preheat your smoker to 225°F(110°C)and prepare it for indirect heat.
Trim any excess fat from the brisket,leaving about 1/4 inch of fat.
Season the brisket with salt and pepper.
In a bowl,combine the maple syrup,Dijon mustard,apple cider vinegar,brown sugar,paprika,garlic powder,onion powder,and cayenne pepper(if using).Mix well.
Rub the maple glaze mixture all over the brisket,making sure to coat all sides.
Place the brisket in the smoker,fat side up.
Close the smoker and let the brisket smoke for about 1.5 to 2 hours per pound,or until the internal temperature reaches around 195°F(90°C)to 203°F(95°C)and the brisket is tender.
Remove the brisket from the smoker and let it rest for at least 30 minutes.
Slice the brisket against the grain and serve.

67. Reverse-Seared Tri-Tip

INGREDIENTS:

$1\frac{1}{2}$pounds tri-tip roast

1 batch Espresso Brisket Rub

INSTRUCTIONS:

a) Season the tri-tip roast with the rub.Using your hands,work the rub into the meat.

b) Place the roast directly on the grill grate and smoke until its internal Smoke Temperature reaches 140°F.

c) Increase the grill's Smoke Temperature to 450°F and continues to cook until the roast's internal Smoke Temperature reaches 145°F.This same technique can be done over an open flame or in a cast-iron skillet with some butter.

d) Remove the tri-tip roast from the grill and let it rest 10 to 15 minutes,before slicing and serving.

GRILLED BRISKET

68.Grilled BBQ Brisket

INGREDIENTS:

1(12-14 Lb.)Whole Packer Brisket

Beef Rub,As Needed

INSTRUCTIONS:

Coat meat liberally with Beef Rub

When seasoned,wrap brisket in plastic wrap.Let the wrapped meat sit 12 to 24 hours in the refrigerator.

Place meat fat side down on the grill grate and cook for 6 hours

Place foiled brisket back on grill and cook until it reaches a finished internal Smoke Temperature of 204 this should take an additional 3-4 hours.

Remove from grill and allow to rest in the foil for at least 30 minutes.Slice.Enjoy!

69.Grilled Teriyaki Brisket

INGREDIENTS:

4-5 pounds beef brisket
1 cup teriyaki sauce
1/4 cup soy sauce
2 tablespoons brown sugar
2 tablespoons sesame oil
2 cloves garlic,minced
Salt and pepper to taste

INSTRUCTIONS:

Preheat your grill to medium heat.

In a bowl,whisk together teriyaki sauce,soy sauce,brown sugar,sesame oil,minced garlic,salt,and pepper.

Place the brisket in a large resealable plastic bag or airtight container and pour the marinade over it.Make sure the brisket is well coated.Marinate in the refrigerator for at least 4 hours,or overnight if possible.

Remove the brisket from the marinade and discard the excess marinade.

Place the brisket on the grill and close the lid.

Cook the brisket for about 1.5 to 2 hours per pound,or until the internal temperature reaches around 195°F(90°C)to 203°F(95°C)and the brisket is tender.

Remove the brisket from the grill and let it rest for at least 30 minutes.

Slice the brisket against the grain and serve.

70.Grilled Brisket Salad

INGREDIENTS:

4-5 pounds beef brisket
Salt and pepper to taste
Mixed salad greens
Cherry tomatoes,halved
Cucumber,sliced
Red onion,thinly sliced
Balsamic vinaigrette or your preferred dressing

INSTRUCTIONS:

Preheat your grill to medium heat.
Season the brisket with salt and pepper.
Place the brisket on the grill and close the lid.
Cook the brisket for about 1.5 to 2 hours per pound,or until the internal temperature reaches around 195°F(90°C)to 203°F(95°C)and the brisket is tender.
Remove the brisket from the grill and let it rest for at least 30 minutes.
Slice the brisket against the grain.
In a large bowl,combine mixed salad greens,cherry tomatoes,cucumber slices,and red onion.
Drizzle with balsamic vinaigrette or your preferred dressing and toss to coat.
Arrange the sliced brisket on top of the salad.
Serve the grilled brisket salad as a delicious and hearty meal.

71. Grilled Brisket Skewers

INGREDIENTS:

4-5 pounds beef brisket,cut into cubes
Salt and pepper to taste
Your favorite marinade or BBQ sauce
Skewers(soaked in water if using wooden skewers)

INSTRUCTIONS:

Preheat your grill to medium heat.
Season the brisket cubes with salt and pepper.
Thread the brisket cubes onto skewers.
Brush the skewered brisket cubes with your favorite marinade or BBQ sauce.
Place the skewers on the grill and close the lid.
Grill for about 10-12 minutes,turning occasionally,or until the brisket is cooked to your desired level of doneness.
Remove the skewers from the grill and let them rest for a few minutes before serving.

72. Grilled Brisket Fajitas

INGREDIENTS:

4-5 pounds beef brisket,sliced into thin strips
Salt and pepper to taste
2 bell peppers,sliced
1 onion,sliced
2 tablespoons olive oil
Fajita seasoning(store-bought or homemade)
Flour tortillas
Toppings:salsa,guacamole,sour cream,shredded cheese,etc.

INSTRUCTIONS:

Preheat your grill to medium heat.
Season the brisket strips with salt,pepper,and fajita seasoning.
In a bowl,toss the sliced bell peppers and onion with olive oil,salt,and pepper.
Place the seasoned brisket strips and the vegetable mixture on the grill.
Grill for about 8-10 minutes,turning the brisket and vegetables occasionally,or until the brisket is cooked to your desired level of doneness and the vegetables are tender.
Remove the brisket and vegetables from the grill and let them rest for a few minutes.
Warm the flour tortillas on the grill.
Assemble the fajitas by placing the grilled brisket and vegetables on the tortillas.
Top with your preferred toppings and fold the tortillas.
Serve the grilled brisket fajitas hot.

73.Grilled Brisket with Chimichurri Sauce

INGREDIENTS:

4-5 pounds beef brisket
Salt and pepper to taste
Chimichurri sauce:
1 cup fresh parsley,finely chopped
1/4 cup fresh cilantro,finely chopped
4 cloves garlic,minced
1/4 cup red wine vinegar
1/4 cup olive oil
1 teaspoon dried oregano
Salt and pepper to taste

INSTRUCTIONS:

Preheat your grill to medium heat.
Season the brisket with salt and pepper.
In a bowl,combine all the ingredients for the chimichurri sauce and mix well.
Place the seasoned brisket on the grill and close the lid.
Grill for about 1.5 to 2 hours per pound,or until the internal temperature reaches around 195°F(90°C)to 203°F(95°C)and the brisket is tender.
Remove the brisket from the grill and let it rest for at least 30 minutes.
Slice the brisket against the grain.
Drizzle the sliced brisket with chimichurri sauce or serve the sauce on the side.
Serve the grilled brisket with chimichurri sauce.

SLOW COOKER/CROCKPOT BRISKET

4.Smoky Slow Cooker Beef Brisket

INGREDIENTS:

- 2 tablespoons extra-virgin olive oil
- 2 tablespoons apple cider vinegar
- 1 tablespoon liquid smoke
- ½cup light brown sugar
- 2 tablespoons garlic powder
- 2 tablespoons onion powder
- 2 tablespoons paprika
- 1 tablespoon kosher salt
- 1 tablespoon dried parsley flakes
- 1 teaspoon ground black pepper
- 1 teaspoon cayenne pepper
- 7 to 8 pounds beef brisket

INSTRUCTIONS

a) In a small mixing bowl,combine the oil,vinegar,liquid smoke,sugar,garlic and onion powders,paprika,salt,parsley,black pepper,and cayenne using a whisk.Rub the mixture all over the brisket.

b) Spray a 6-quart slow cooker with nonstick cooking spray and place the brisket inside.Set the slow cooker on low and cook for 12 hours.

c) Line a 9-by-13-inch baking dish with aluminum foil.Once the brisket is done,carefully remove it from the slow cooker and place it in the prepared baking dish.Turn the oven on broil and cook the brisket until the"bark"(the rub)is dark brown,3 to 5 minutes.Remove the brisket from the oven,cover it with aluminum foil,and let it rest for 1 hour before serving.

75.Slow Cooker brisket

INGREDIENTS:

- 4 pounds of beef brisket
- 3 tablespoons of flour
- Salt and pepper

INSTRUCTIONS:

a) Cook on low for 6 hours at 250 degrees.

b) Mix the juice,flour,salt,and pepper to make the sauce,and drizzle the sauce over the brisket.

76.Slow Cooker Brisket Tacos

INGREDIENTS:

3-4 pounds beef brisket
1 onion,sliced
4 cloves garlic,minced
1 jalapeno pepper,seeded and diced
1 tablespoon chili powder
1 teaspoon ground cumin
1 teaspoon paprika
1/2 teaspoon oregano
Salt and pepper to taste
Corn tortillas
Toppings:chopped cilantro,diced onion,sliced radishes,lime wedges,salsa,etc.

INSTRUCTIONS:

Season the brisket with salt,pepper,chili powder,cumin,paprika,and oregano.
Place the sliced onion,minced garlic,and jalapeno pepper in the slow cooker.
Place the seasoned brisket on top of the vegetables.
Cover the slow cooker and cook on low for 8-10 hours or on high for 4-6 hours,until the brisket is tender and easily shreds.
Remove the brisket from the slow cooker and shred it using two forks.
Warm the corn tortillas and fill them with the shredded brisket.
Serve the tacos with your desired toppings.

7. Slow Cooker Brisket and Gravy

INGREDIENTS:

3-4 pounds beef brisket
1 onion,sliced
4 cloves garlic,minced
1 cup beef broth
1/4 cup soy sauce
2 tablespoons Worcestershire sauce
1 tablespoon Dijon mustard
2 tablespoons cornstarch(optional,for thickening)
Salt and pepper to taste

INSTRUCTIONS:

Season the brisket with salt and pepper.
Place the sliced onion and minced garlic in the slow cooker.
Place the seasoned brisket on top of the onions and garlic.
In a bowl,mix together beef broth,soy sauce,Worcestershire sauce,and Dijon mustard.Pour the mixture over the brisket.
Cover the slow cooker and cook on low for 8-10 hours or on high for 4-6 hours,until the brisket is tender.
Once cooked,remove the brisket from the slow cooker and let it rest for a few minutes.
If desired,thicken the cooking liquid by mixing cornstarch with a small amount of water,then stirring it into the liquid in the slow cooker.Cook on high for an additional 15-20 minutes or until thickened.
Slice the brisket against the grain and serve with the gravy.

78.Slow Cooker Brisket Chili

INGREDIENTS:

3-4 pounds beef brisket,trimmed and cut into cubes
1 onion,diced
3 cloves garlic,minced
1 jalapeno pepper,seeded and diced
1 can(14 ounces)diced tomatoes
1 can(14 ounces)kidney beans,drained and rinsed
1 can(14 ounces)black beans,drained and rinsed
2 tablespoons chili powder
1 tablespoon ground cumin
1 teaspoon paprika
1/2 teaspoon oregano
Salt and pepper to taste
Optional toppings:shredded cheese,sour cream,chopped cilantro,diced onion,etc.

INSTRUCTIONS:

a) Season the brisket cubes with salt,pepper,chili powder,cumin,paprika,and oregano.
b) Place the seasoned brisket,diced onion,minced garlic,jalapeno pepper,diced tomatoes,kidney beans,and black beans in the slow cooker.
c) Cover the slow cooker and cook on low for 8-10 hours or on high for 4-6 hours,until the brisket is tender and the flavors meld together.
d) Once cooked,taste and adjust the seasoning if needed.
e) Serve the brisket chili in bowls and top with your desired toppings.

79.Crockpot brisket

INGREDIENTS:

- 4 pounds of beef brisket
- 3 tablespoons of flour
- Salt and pepper

INSTRUCTIONS:

a) Cook on low for 6 hours at 250 degrees.
b) Mix the juice,flour,salt,and pepper to make the sauce,and drizzle the sauce over the brisket.

0.Slow Cooker Brisket with Red Wine Sauce

INGREDIENTS:

3-4 pounds beef brisket
1 onion,sliced
4 cloves garlic,minced
1 cup red wine
1 cup beef broth
2 tablespoons tomato paste
2 tablespoons brown sugar
1 tablespoon Dijon mustard
Salt and pepper to taste

INSTRUCTIONS:

Season the brisket with salt and pepper.
Place the sliced onion and minced garlic in the slow cooker.
Place the seasoned brisket on top of the onions and garlic.
In a bowl,mix together red wine,beef broth,tomato paste,brown sugar,and Dijon mustard.Pour the mixture over the brisket.
Cover the slow cooker and cook on low for 8-10 hours or on high for 4-6 hours,until the brisket is tender.
Once cooked,remove the brisket from the slow cooker and let it rest for a few minutes.
Strain the cooking liquid into a saucepan and simmer over medium heat until it reduces and thickens to desired consistency.
Slice the brisket against the grain and serve with the red wine sauce.

SOUS VIDE BRISKET

81. Sous Vide Corned Beef

INGREDIENTS:

- 1(5-pound)beef brisket
- 1 cup dark beer
- 1 cup beef stock
- 2 tablespoons pickling spice
- 1 onion,sliced
- 1 head cabbage(optional)

INSTRUCTIONS:

a) Set your Anova to 135F/57.2C.

b) Rub the brisket with pickling spice and place in a vacuum-sealed bag with the beer,beef stock,and onion.

c) Seal the bag and submerge in the water bath for 48 hours.

d) Remove from the water bath and slice against the grain.

e) Bonus:If you want to accompany your corned beef with braised cabbage,remove the brisket from the bag and replace with chopped cabbage.

f) Mix with the cooking liquid and use your Foodsaver to reseal the bag.Submerge in the water bath for 30 minutes and serve.

82. Sous Vide Barbecue Beef Brisket

INGREDIENTS:

- 1(5-pound)beef brisket
- 4 tablespoons ground cumin
- 2 tablespoons smoked paprika
- 2 tablespoons dry mustard
- 3 tablespoons dark brown sugar
- 2 tablespoons ground rosemary
- 1 tablespoon cayenne pepper
- 3 tablespoons salt
- 1 cup your favorite barbecue sauce
- 2 teaspoons liquid smoke

INSTRUCTIONS:

a) Set your Anova to 137F/58.3C.
b) In a bowl,combine the cumin,paprika,mustard,sugar,rosemary,pepper,and salt.
c) Rub the spice blend all over the brisket and place in the refrigerator for one hour.
d) Remove the brisket from the refrigerator and coat,liberally,with half of the barbecue sauce.
e) Place the brisket in a vacuum-sealed bag and submerge in the water bath for 24 to 48 hours.
f) When the brisket is nearly finished cooking,heat your oven to 450F.
g) Remove the brisket from the water bath,coat with the remaining barbecue sauce and cook in the oven for 10 minutes.
h) Slice the brisket thinly against the grain and serve.

83. Sous Vide Pulled Beef

INGREDIENTS:

- 2 pounds beef brisket
- 4 sprigs of thyme
- 1 tablespoon olive oil
- 2 cloves garlic,smashed
- 1 bay leaf
- 1 yellow onion,chopped
- 1 large ancho chili,seeded and split
- 1 tablespoon tomato paste
- 1 tablespoon salt
- 1/4 cup your favorite barbecue sauce
- 4 Kaiser rolls or hamburger buns

INSTRUCTIONS:

a) Set your Anova to 185F/85C.

b) In a large cast iron pan,heat the oil over medium-high heat and sear the brisket on all sides.

c) In a vacuum-sealed bag,combine the beef,thyme,garlic,bay leaf,onion,chili,tomato paste,and salt.Seal and submerge in the water bath for 24 hours.

d) Remove the bag from the water bath and remove the beef from the bag,discarding all other ingredients.

e) Place the beef in a large bowl and shred with forks.

f) Serve on the rolls with a generous spoonful of barbecue sauce.

84. Sous Vide Smoked Brisket

INGREDIENTS:

4-5 pounds beef brisket
Salt and pepper to taste
Your favorite dry rub
Wood chips for smoking(such as hickory or mesquite)

INSTRUCTIONS:

Preheat your water bath or sous vide immersion circulator to 155°F(68°C).
Season the brisket with salt,pepper,and your favorite dry rub,ensuring it is evenly coated.
Place the seasoned brisket in a vacuum-sealed bag or a sturdy resealable plastic bag.
Seal the bag using a vacuum sealer or the water displacement method.
Submerge the bag in the preheated water bath and cook for 24 to 48 hours.
Once the cooking time is complete,remove the bag from the water bath and let the brisket rest for a few minutes.
Preheat your smoker to 225°F(110°C)and prepare it for indirect heat.
Remove the brisket from the bag and pat it dry with paper towels.
Place the brisket in the smoker and smoke it for 2 to 3 hours,adding wood chips for smoke flavor.
Remove the brisket from the smoker and let it rest for at least 30 minutes.
Slice the brisket against the grain and serve.

85.Sous Vide Red Wine Braised Brisket

INGREDIENTS:

4-5 pounds beef brisket
Salt and pepper to taste
2 cups red wine
1 cup beef broth
2 onions,sliced
4 cloves garlic,minced
2 carrots,chopped
2 celery stalks,chopped
2 sprigs fresh rosemary
2 sprigs fresh thyme

INSTRUCTIONS:

Preheat your water bath or sous vide immersion circulator to 155°F(68°C).

Season the brisket with salt and pepper.

Place the seasoned brisket in a vacuum-sealed bag or a sturdy resealable plastic bag.

In a separate bowl,combine red wine,beef broth,sliced onions,minced garlic,chopped carrots,chopped celery,rosemary,and thyme.

Pour the red wine mixture into the bag with the brisket.

Seal the bag using a vacuum sealer or the water displacement method.

Submerge the bag in the preheated water bath and cook for 24 to 48 hours.

Once the cooking time is complete,remove the bag from the water bath and let the brisket rest for a few minutes.

Remove the brisket from the bag,reserving the cooking liquid.

Preheat a large skillet or Dutch oven over medium-high heat.

Sear the brisket on all sides until browned.

Strain the cooking liquid and discard the solids.

Add the strained liquid to the skillet or Dutch oven with the seared brisket.

Reduce the heat to low,cover,and simmer for 1 to 2 hours,until the brisket is tender and the sauce has thickened.

Slice the brisket against the grain and serve with the braising sauce.

86. Sous Vide Asian-Style Brisket

INGREDIENTS:

4-5 pounds beef brisket
Salt and pepper to taste
1/2 cup soy sauce
1/4 cup hoisin sauce
2 tablespoons honey
2 tablespoons rice vinegar
2 cloves garlic,minced
1 tablespoon grated ginger

INSTRUCTIONS:

Preheat your water bath or sous vide immersion circulator to 155°F(68°C).

Season the brisket with salt and pepper.

In a bowl,whisk together soy sauce,hoisin sauce,honey,rice vinegar,minced garlic,and grated ginger.

Place the seasoned brisket in a vacuum-sealed bag or a sturdy resealable plastic bag.

Pour the Asian-style sauce into the bag with the brisket.

Seal the bag using a vacuum sealer or the water displacement method.

Submerge the bag in the preheated water bath and cook for 24 to 48 hours.

Once the cooking time is complete,remove the bag from the water bath and let the brisket rest for a few minutes.

Preheat your grill or broiler to high heat.

Remove the brisket from the bag and pat it dry with paper towels.

Grill or broil the brisket for a few minutes on each side,until it develops a nice crust.

Slice the brisket against the grain and serve.

DUTCH OVEN BRISKET

87.Dutch Oven Barbecued Brisket

INGREDIENTS:

- 3 cups apple cider
- $\frac{1}{4}$cups honey
- 2 tablespoons Dijon mustard
- $\frac{1}{4}$cup soy sauce
- 2 tablespoons brown sugar,packed
- 1 tablespoon minced garlic
- 1 tablespoon minced fresh ginger root
- 1 tablespoon whole coriander
- 2 sprigs fresh thyme
- 1 brisket of beef(2$\frac{1}{2}$pounds)
- 1 cup white wine(optional)

INSTRUCTIONS:

a) Combine,white wine,cider,honey,mustard,soy sauce,brown sugar,garlic,ginger root,coriander and thyme in Dutch oven.

b) Add brisket.Cover tightly and place in oven.Heat oven to 350 degrees F and cook 1 hour.

c) Remove brisket from cooking liquid,cover and set aside.

d) Transfer liquid to medium pan and cook over medium heat until reduced to a glaze and thick enough

e) to coat back of spoon.Using covered grill,light about 12 charcoal briquettes and add small piece of mesquite or other wood.Be sure to place charcoal and wood to one side of grill.

f) Arrange brisket on grill so that it is not directly over burning wood.Paint it with some glaze.

g) Place cover on grill and smoke brisket 1 hour,turning meat and coating with glaze every 15 minutes.Add charcoal or wood,small piece at a time,if fire seems to get too cold.

h) Remove from grill,thinly slice meat against grain and serve.

i) Offer any remaining glaze on side.

88. Dutch Oven Macaroni and Beef Brisket

INGREDIENTS:

- 2½to 3 pounds beef brisket
- 1 12-ounce package macaroni
- water(you can add tomato juice or beef stock to water if you like)

INSTRUCTIONS:

a) Place Dutch oven directly on coals and add a little oil or shorting.

b) Add brisket and brown well on both sides.Add water to almost cover the brisket.

c) Cover oven and place coals on the oven lid and cook until meat is tender,about two hours.

d) Remove meat from cooking juices and wrap in foil to keep warm.

e) Add macaroni to cooking juices and place oven directly on hot coals.

f) Boil,uncovered until pasta is tender,about 20 minutes.

39. Dutch Oven Smoked Brisket

INGREDIENTS:

4-5 pounds beef brisket
Salt and pepper to taste
Your favorite dry rub
Wood chips for smoking(such as hickory or mesquite)

INSTRUCTIONS:

Preheat your oven to 225°F(110°C).
Season the brisket with salt,pepper,and your favorite dry rub,ensuring it is evenly coated.
Heat a Dutch oven over medium-high heat on the stovetop.
Place the brisket in the Dutch oven and sear it on all sides until browned.
Remove the brisket from the Dutch oven and set it aside.
Line the bottom of the Dutch oven with aluminum foil and place a handful of wood chips on top.
Return the brisket to the Dutch oven,fat side up.
Cover the Dutch oven with a lid and transfer it to the preheated oven.
Smoke the brisket in the Dutch oven for about 6 to 8 hours,or until the internal temperature reaches around 195°F(90°C)to 203°F(95°C)and the brisket is tender.
Remove the Dutch oven from the oven and let the brisket rest for a few minutes.
Slice the brisket against the grain and serve.

0.Dutch Oven Brisket with Mushroom Gravy

INGREDIENTS:

4-5 pounds beef brisket
Salt and pepper to taste
2 tablespoons vegetable oil
2 onions,sliced
8 ounces mushrooms,sliced
4 cloves garlic,minced
2 cups beef broth
1 cup red wine(optional)
2 tablespoons all-purpose flour
Fresh herbs such as rosemary and thyme

INSTRUCTIONS:

Preheat your oven to 325°F(165°C).

Season the brisket with salt and pepper.

Heat the vegetable oil in a Dutch oven over medium-high heat.

Brown the brisket on all sides in the Dutch oven.Remove the brisket from the Dutch oven and set it aside.

In the same Dutch oven,add the sliced onions,sliced mushrooms,and minced garlic.Cook until softened and lightly browned.

Sprinkle the flour over the vegetables and stir to coat.

Deglaze the Dutch oven with the beef broth and red wine(if using),scraping up any browned bits from the bottom.

Return the brisket to the Dutch oven and add fresh herbs.

Cover the Dutch oven with a lid and transfer it to the preheated oven.

Braise the brisket for about 3 to 4 hours,or until it is tender and easily shreds with a fork.

Remove the Dutch oven from the oven and let the brisket rest for a few minutes.

Slice the brisket against the grain and serve with the mushroom gravy.

91.Dutch Oven Brisket Chili

INGREDIENTS:

4-5 pounds beef brisket,cubed
Salt and pepper to taste
2 tablespoons vegetable oil
1 onion,diced
2 bell peppers,diced
4 cloves garlic,minced
2 cans(14 ounces each)diced tomatoes
2 cans(15 ounces each)kidney beans,drained and rinsed
2 tablespoons chili powder
1 tablespoon ground cumin
1 teaspoon paprika
1/2 teaspoon cayenne pepper(optional)
1 cup beef broth
Fresh cilantro,chopped(for garnish)

INSTRUCTIONS:

Preheat your oven to 325°F(165°C).

Season the brisket cubes with salt and pepper.

Heat the vegetable oil in a Dutch oven over medium-high heat.

Brown the brisket cubes in the Dutch oven.Remove the brisket from the Dutch oven and set it aside.

In the same Dutch oven,add the diced onion,diced bell peppers,and minced garlic.Cook until softened.

Add the diced tomatoes,kidney beans,chili powder,ground cumin,paprika,cayenne pepper(if using),and beef broth to the Dutch oven.Stir to combine.

Return the brisket to the Dutch oven and stir to coat with the chili mixture.

Cover the Dutch oven with a lid and transfer it to the preheated oven.
Cook the chili for about 2 to 3 hours,or until the brisket is tender and the flavors have melded together.
Remove the Dutch oven from the oven and let the chili rest for a few minutes.
Serve the brisket chili hot,garnished with fresh cilantro.

2. Dutch Oven Brisket Stew

INGREDIENTS:

- 4-5 pounds beef brisket,cubed
- Salt and pepper to taste
- 2 tablespoons vegetable oil
- 2 onions,diced
- 4 cloves garlic,minced
- 4 carrots,chopped
- 4 celery stalks,chopped
- 2 potatoes,peeled and diced
- 2 cups beef broth
- 1 cup red wine(optional)
- 2 tablespoons tomato paste
- 2 tablespoons Worcestershire sauce
- Fresh herbs such as rosemary and thyme

INSTRUCTIONS:

a) Preheat your oven to 325°F(165°C).
b) Season the brisket cubes with salt and pepper.
c) Heat the vegetable oil in a Dutch oven over medium-high heat.
d) Brown the brisket cubes in the Dutch oven.Remove the brisket from the Dutch oven and set it aside.
e) In the same Dutch oven,add the diced onions,minced garlic,chopped carrots,chopped celery,and diced potatoes.Cook until softened.
f) Return the brisket to the Dutch oven.
g) In a separate bowl,whisk together the beef broth,red wine(if using),tomato paste,and Worcestershire sauce.Pour the mixture over the brisket and vegetables in the Dutch oven.
h) Add fresh herbs to the Dutch oven.

i) Cover the Dutch oven with a lid and transfer it to the preheated oven.
j) Cook the stew for about 2 to 3 hours,or until the brisket is tender and the flavors have melded together.
k) Remove the Dutch oven from the oven and let the stew rest for a few minutes.
l) Serve the brisket stew hot.

93.Dutch Oven Brisket and Potatoes

INGREDIENTS:

4-5 pounds beef brisket
Salt and pepper to taste
2 tablespoons vegetable oil
2 onions,sliced
4 cloves garlic,minced
2 pounds potatoes,peeled and cut into chunks
2 cups beef broth
Fresh herbs such as rosemary and thyme

INSTRUCTIONS:

Preheat your oven to 325°F(165°C).

Season the brisket with salt and pepper.

Heat the vegetable oil in a Dutch oven over medium-high heat.

Brown the brisket on all sides in the Dutch oven.Remove the brisket from the Dutch oven and set it aside.

In the same Dutch oven,add the sliced onions and minced garlic.Cook until softened and lightly browned.

Return the brisket to the Dutch oven and add the potato chunks.

Pour the beef broth over the brisket and potatoes in the Dutch oven.

Add fresh herbs to the Dutch oven.

Cover the Dutch oven with a lid and transfer it to the preheated oven.

Braise the brisket and potatoes for about 3 to 4 hours,or until the brisket is tender and easily shreds with a fork,and the potatoes are cooked through.

Remove the Dutch oven from the oven and let the brisket and potatoes rest for a few minutes.

Slice the brisket against the grain and serve with the potatoes and cooking liquid.

CONDIMENTS

94. Homemade Pickles

INGREDIENTS:

- 2 pounds pickling cucumbers
- 1 cup white vinegar
- 1 cup water
- 1/4 cup granulated sugar
- 2 tablespoons kosher salt
- 2 cloves garlic,smashed
- 1 tablespoon dill seeds
- 1 teaspoon black peppercorns
- 1/2 teaspoon mustard seeds
- Fresh dill sprigs(optional)

INSTRUCTIONS:

a) Wash the cucumbers thoroughly and slice them into rounds or spears.
b) In a saucepan,combine the vinegar,water,sugar,salt,garlic,dill seeds,black peppercorns,and mustard seeds.
c) Place the saucepan over medium heat and bring the mixture to a boil.Stir until the sugar and salt have dissolved.
d) Remove the saucepan from the heat and let the brine cool for about 10 minutes.
e) Pack the sliced cucumbers into clean jars.
f) Pour the brine over the cucumbers,ensuring they are fully submerged.
g) Add fresh dill sprigs to the jars,if desired.
h) Seal the jars and refrigerate for at least 24 hours before using.
i) The pickles will keep in the refrigerator for several weeks.

95. Chimichurri

INGREDIENTS:

1 cup fresh parsley leaves,chopped
1/4 cup fresh cilantro leaves,chopped
3 cloves garlic,minced
1/2 cup olive oil
2 tablespoons red wine vinegar
1 teaspoon dried oregano
1/2 teaspoon red pepper flakes
Salt and black pepper to taste

INSTRUCTIONS:

In a bowl,combine the parsley,cilantro,garlic,olive oil,red wine vinegar,dried oregano,red pepper flakes,salt,and black pepper.
Stir well to combine.
Let the chimichurri sit for at least 30 minutes before serving to allow the flavors to meld.
Store any leftovers in an airtight container in the refrigerator.

96. Chipotle Sauce

INGREDIENTS:

2 chipotle peppers in adobo sauce
1/2 cup mayonnaise
2 tablespoons lime juice
1 clove garlic,minced
Salt to taste

INSTRUCTIONS:

In a blender or food processor,combine the chipotle peppers,mayonnaise,lime juice,garlic,and salt.
Blend until smooth.
Taste and adjust the seasoning if needed.
Transfer the sauce to a jar or airtight container and refrigerate.

97.Hot BBQ Sauce

INGREDIENTS:

- 1 cup ketchup
- 1/4 cup brown sugar
- 2 tablespoons hot sauce of your choice
- 2 tablespoons apple cider vinegar
- 1 tablespoon Worcestershire sauce
- 1 teaspoon smoked paprika
- 1/2 teaspoon garlic powder
- 1/2 teaspoon onion powder
- 1/4 teaspoon cayenne pepper(optional for extra heat)

INSTRUCTIONS:

In a saucepan,combine all the ingredients and whisk together until well combined.

Heat the sauce over medium heat,stirring occasionally,until it comes to a simmer.

Reduce the heat to low and let the sauce simmer for about 10 minutes to allow the flavors to meld.

Remove from heat and let the sauce cool.

Transfer the sauce to a jar or airtight container and refrigerate.

98.Hot Garlic Sauce

INGREDIENTS:

8 cloves garlic, minced
1/4 cup olive oil
2 tablespoons hot sauce of your choice
1 tablespoon lemon juice
1/2 teaspoon salt

INSTRUCTIONS:

In a small saucepan, heat the olive oil over medium heat.
Add the minced garlic and sauté for 2-3 minutes until fragrant and lightly golden.
Remove from heat and let the garlic cool slightly.
In a bowl, combine the sautéed garlic, hot sauce, lemon juice, and salt.
Stir well to combine.
Transfer the sauce to a jar or airtight container and refrigerate.

99.Hot Georgia BBQ Sauce

INGREDIENTS:

1 cup ketchup
1/4 cup apple cider vinegar
2 tablespoons molasses
2 tablespoons hot sauce of your choice
1 tablespoon Dijon mustard
1 tablespoon Worcestershire sauce
1 teaspoon smoked paprika
1/2 teaspoon garlic powder
1/2 teaspoon onion powder
1/4 teaspoon cayenne pepper (optional for extra heat)

INSTRUCTIONS:

In a saucepan, combine all the ingredients and whisk together until well combined.

Heat the sauce over medium heat, stirring occasionally, until it comes to a simmer.

Reduce the heat to low and let the sauce simmer for about 10 minutes to allow the flavors to meld.

Remove from heat and let the sauce cool.

Transfer the sauce to a jar or airtight container and refrigerate.

100. Smoky Sriracha Hot Sauce

INGREDIENTS:

1 cup red chili peppers (deseeded and chopped)
4 cloves garlic (minced)
1/4 cup distilled vinegar
2 tablespoons smoked paprika
1 tablespoon sugar
1 tablespoon salt

INSTRUCTIONS:

Blend the chili peppers, garlic, vinegar, smoked paprika, sugar, and salt in a food processor until smooth.
Pour the mixture into a saucepan and simmer over low heat for 15-20 minutes, stirring occasionally.
Allow the sauce to cool completely, then transfer it to a jar or bottle and store it in the refrigerator.

CONCLUSION

We've reached the end of "BRISKET DISHES COOKBOOK " We hope this cookbook has inspired you to explore the wonders of brisket and discover new ways to enjoy this beloved cut of meat. From the first bite to the last, we've shared recipes that celebrate the rich flavors and textures that brisket has to offer.

Remember, cooking brisket is an art that requires patience, practice, and a love for good food. Whether you're hosting a backyard barbecue, a festive gathering, or simply preparing a comforting meal for yourself, these recipes will be your guide to creating exceptional brisket dishes every time.

As you continue your culinary adventures, don't be afraid to experiment and add your own personal touch to these recipes. Let your creativity shine, and make each dish uniquely yours. With each smoky aroma and melt-in-your-mouth bite, savor the joy that comes from sharing great food with loved ones.

Thank you for joining us on this flavorful journey. May your brisket always be tender, your flavors always bold, and your taste buds forever satisfied. Happy cooking!

Milton Keynes UK
Ingram Content Group UK Ltd.
UKHW020758061023
430068UK00014B/662

9 781835 647370